Our Busy Lives

Clare Hibbert

Illustrated by Silvia Raga

TULIP
BOOKS®

www.tulipbooks.co.uk

This edition published by:
© Tulip Books 2014

First published in this edition by Evans Brothers Ltd, London in 2011.

Concept: Clare Hibbert
Educational consultants: Sue Palmer, Josephine Hussey
Editor: Clare Hibbert
Designer: Sandra Perry
Illustrator: Silvia Raga (Milan Illustration Agency)

British Library Cataloguing in Publication Data (CIP) is available for this title.

ISBN 978-1-78388-049-2

Printed in Spain by Edelvives

The website addresses on page 22 are correct at the time of going to print but the
publisher cannot be held responsible for changes to website addresses or content.

Contents

Everyone starts life as a baby. This is my cousin, Josh.

Babies

GURGLE GURGLE

rattle

baby

blanket

bouncer

Our cat has had babies too. They're called kittens.

I'm at the zoo with my sister. She's a toddler. She can walk, but she wobbles a bit.

First steps

camera

sunhat

I started school this year. I've made lots of new friends! And I'm learning to read.

Starting school

railings

school bag

new shoes

8

Mum

school

CHATTER
CHATTER

These children in Africa have just started school, too.

When I'm a teenager I'll start shaving. I watch my big brother Tom when he shaves.

Growing up

mirror

soap

dressing
gown

razor

BZZZZZZZ!

Jewish boys have a party called a bar mitzvah when they're 13.

11

Today we're taking our cat to the vet's. When I grow up I want to be a vet.

Doing a job

carry case

12

13

I'm dressed up very smart for Uncle's wedding. I'm the pageboy!

Getting married

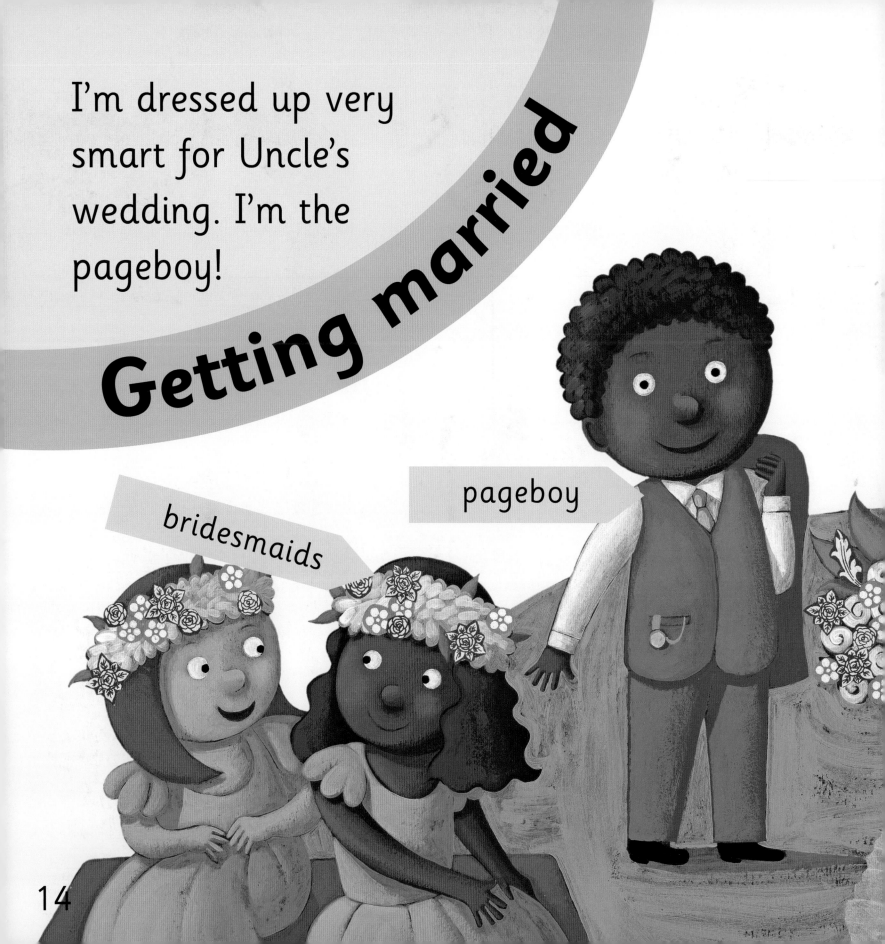

bridesmaids

pageboy

14

groom

bride

flowers

DING! DONG!

Our neighbours had their wedding in a temple.

Mum is having another baby soon, so we're moving to a new house.

Moving house

car

moving van

old flat

HEAVE!

23

sofa

HEAVE!

If I were a tortoise, I could carry my house on my back!

17

Today Auntie Tina's coming to the village fete. She's too old to work, but she keeps busy!

Growing old

ice-cream seller

BRR

18

bric-a-brac stall

scooter

One day I'll be old, too. I might be a grandad!

19

I miss Grandpa, who died last year. I like to look at photos of us together.

Remembering life

album

Notes for adults

The **Busy Times** series links in to the Early Years Foundation Stage curriculum and beyond. The series provides useful resources for exploring time in accordance with the Early Years Foundation Stage Practice Guidance from birth to five.

In today's fast-paced world, it's more important than ever to talk with young children about the passage of 'real time'. Television programmes, films and games often confuse children – for example, by using cutting techniques that telescope time passing.

The series supports young children as they begin to grasp the complex concept of time. It looks at how we mark specific moments, and how children can come to predict the order of routine events. Although children do not tell the time at this stage, they will enjoy hunting for the hidden clocks and watches.

In order to introduce the passing of time in an age-appropriate way, every spread in the **Busy Times** books illustrates a moment in a child's day, week, year or life.

As you explore the books together, you can use the pages to link in with the specifics of the child reader's life. Discuss what he or she does at those particular times. Which settings are familiar favourites? Which activities are new or unfamiliar?

Each spread also has a unique 'Window on the World' feature. Through this, children can glimpse something else happening at the same time as the main action on the spread – another, concurrent event. The window is really useful for broadening children's perspective, helping them to understand that things go on even when they are not there.

USEFUL WEBSITES

Department for Education	www.education.gov.uk
National Literacy Trust	www.literacytrust.org.uk
Early Years resources	www.earlyyearsresources.co.uk, www.under5s.com

Reading with younger children

As you read, allow quiet spaces so that children can ask questions or repeat your words. Try pausing mid-sentence so that children can predict the next word. This sort of participation gives a sense of achievement and develops early reading skills.

Follow the words with your finger. The main text in the **Busy Times** books is in Infant Sassoon, a clear, friendly font designed for children learning to read and write. The sound effects add fun and introduce readers to different levels of communication.

Take time to explore the pictures together. Ask children to find, identify, count or describe different objects — not just the hidden timepieces. Point out colours and textures. The illustration style in the **Busy Times** series is especially rich and rewarding.

Children delight in repetition; they also need to revisit complex concepts on a regular basis. Expect to share these books time after time. There is lots of scope in the pictures for many different conversations.

Use the Busy Life spreads as a springboard for extension activities:

• Encourage children to paint themselves as a baby, young child, teenager, adult and elderly person. Why not cut up the image to turn it into a jigsaw?

• Help children to make a height chart for recording their growth over time. 'The Growing Story' by Ruth Krauss is a lovely picture book on this subject.

• Practise chanting the traditional rhyme 'Solomon Grundy'. It teaches the days of the week, as well as covering the key moments in Solomon's life.

• Complement children's understanding of human life events by looking at non-fiction books about baby animals and how they grow and develop.

Talking about death with young children

The final spread aims to introduce the concept of death in a sensitive way. Look on the Internet or in your local library or bookshop for resources offering detailed guidance on answering children's questions. You'll also find recommendations for picture books that explore death in an age-appropriate way.

Index